# Reflections on the Eternal lover

# Reflections on the Eternal lover

*A young women's poetry collection on God in life*

## Christina Carpenter

authorHOUSE®

*AuthorHouse™*
*1663 Liberty Drive*
*Bloomington, IN 47403*
*www.authorhouse.com*
*Phone: 1-800-839-8640*

*First published by AuthorHouse    09/30/2011*

*ISBN: 978-1-4634-4569-0 (sc)*
*ISBN: 978-1-4634-4568-3 (ebk)*

*Library of Congress Control Number: 2011913610*

*Printed in the United States of America*

# CONTENTS

Get ready to reflect and experience 40 poems in 40 days . . . 40 days is not long at all! Especially when it involves God, life and poetry, it's a great time!

# ACKNOWLEDGMENTS

This book is dedicated to four individuals.

First of all my **God**, My eternal lover, without Him, this book would not be existent and I would not be who I am.

Reggie Carpenter, my beloved Father. He is with the Lord but is always my driving force of inspiration.

Connie and Caren, my family. They surround me with love, joy and hopeful days of fun and direction for life.

# INTRODUCTION

These poems came from reflections and revelations on God in my life. In a large part every poem is about God, life, love, and hope. Because without God there is no life, love or hope. I share these poems with you.

Starting with the title, God is our Eternal Lover. For God so loved that world that he gave his only son . . . That comes from John 3:16. God loves us and has the best for us and he promised it. He sent his Son, Jesus Christ, to be our Savior. Because of Jesus we have Hope and Life. This is only the beginning of the story.

As you will find ahead, this poetry collection is all about life. Please feel free to flip back and forth from the poems you like and to the reflections, at the end of the book, that correspond to it. These questions are for deeper reflections, relevant to each poem. They are to get you thinking and reflecting; pondering deeper issues.

Hopefully you will be able to learn and even identify with the revelations. Be encouraged and grow in your love for the Lord. God's love brings me hope. This hope is meant to be shared and I am excited to share my poetry with you.

This book is in a 40 day format. But don't hesitate to read it in more than 40 days! Read at leisure and begin to have your own reflections!

<u>Find a chair, relax, and enjoy!!</u>

# PROLOGUE

## SEPERATION

Lives with no purpose, no direction, meaningless

We had a price to pay

A noose hanging over our heads

We didn't even know it.

For every wrong we committed

It was ready to take our breath away

Paying the price because of our sins.

No one was right, no one good enough

Though we pretended to be

Pleaded and acted, but fooled no one.

No one pleased God

Not till Grace came

When Jesus paid it all,

Shed his blood

No longer do we need to lie or die

Separated from hope and eternal life.

Now we can turn to the light,

To the cross

Accept the love of Jesus Christ

Given by our father God, for us all

No one can be against us

Now, his only son is for us

He took our sin, our guilt, and our condemnation

So that we are one

In purpose and in journey

No longer alone

No longer separated, no longer clueless

To the hope and the grace of God's forgiveness.

By Christina Carpenter

7/15/11


*"Who shall separate us from the love of Christ? "Romans 8:35 NIV*


*"I have loved you with an everlasting love; I have drawn you with loving kindness." Jeremiah 31:3NIV*

# PART 1

---

## RELATIONSHIP TO THE
## ETERNAL LOVER

---

*But seek ye first the kingdom of God, and his righteousness; and all these things shall be added unto you.* Matthew 6:33 KJV

*Reminder: check out the additional reflections at the end of this book in the appendix.*

# *Day 1*

---

My soul finds rest in God alone; my salvation comes from him. He alone is my rock and my salvation; he is my fortress, I will never be shaken.

Psalm 62:1-2 NIV

## REMEMBERING GOD AND

## PRACTICING HIS PRESENCE

Sometimes,

I like to lay down in my blue bed and

Think of happy times.

I praise God for how He has been good and faithful to me.

I smile and hug Him with my mind.

I clasp my hands as if to shake His hands.

I feel my pulse beating quick yet in the stillness,

I am reminded of His love and control.

By Christina Carpenter

Written 8/ 20/2009

*Reminder: check out the additional reflections at the end of this book in the appendix.*

# Day 2

## TO KNOW YOU . . . IS TO KNOW LOVE.

God is love . . . and love caste out all fear

His love goes on . . . . forever

Beyond the horizon of the sea

Farther than the eye can see

He will always love me and continues loving me

He shows unconditional love

And He will never let go

Never will God ever let me go.

Christina Carpenter Written 11/9/04

## REFLECTIONS ON THE ETERNAL LOVER

*This is the love . . .*
*God's love to me.*
On *any given day* or time or season
That I might see
And be **reminded** that He is
And always will be.
The *smile* on a rainy day.
The *sunshine*
Through my windowpane.
*Golden rays* and Rainbow prisms
—sprinkled on my carpet floor.
*Meeting* a cherished friend
From long—long ago.


Sudden *opportunities* where
There were none before.
An *unexpected* warm glow

In the heart and on the face,

When there was no reason at all.

Having much more *time*

When the clock almost stopped ticking.

Having *sudden* determination

When all hope had seemed lost

The *kindness* of a stranger

In a sea of angry Faces

The *speech* of a good friend

That pieces Back the heart

*Together again*

Just what is needed . . . At the right *time*

On the right *day.*

And in the right *way.*


These are the things **I've Seen**

The good things of life

Every good thing

And all these simple little things

They come from above.

At the perfect good time.

It is from my Father above

***Though* God *is unseen***

I have seen **His love**.


By Christina Carpenter Written 2/8/2005

## I WILL CALL ALOUD TO YOU

When I have no one beside me
I will call on you when I am afraid
I will call on you when I feel worthless
You give me my worth.

Your love comes over me like a rushing wind
Blowing my face
Blowing my hair
I am engulfed by your pure presence
So holy are you God and yet you
Converse with me so little and unworthy
But that is who you are—you love the least
And make them the greatest.

Thank you for lifting me up and making
Me to soar with you

Grace, healed, delivered and saved

By the blood of the lamb

Thank you for being the lamb

The precious sacrificial lamb

So willing, so missive, so humble

How great you are

Oh lord.


I praise you lord

*For Who You Are.*


By: Christina Carpenter 2008

Day 5

## GOD'S MERCY AND GOD'S GRACE

God hears, God sees and God knows everything

The things we've done that cause guilt

The things we've done that cause shame

Yet God in his mercy forgives us

And yet God in his mercy heals us from our past

So we need not feel guilt or shame

He is making our scarlet robes

As pure white snow.

So we thank God for his mercy,

And we thank God for his grace,

Because he has allowed us to no longer hide our face.

By Christina Carpenter 1/14/03

## TRUST GOD TO BE . . .

Trust in God to be your Hope and Strength,

To pick you up when you've fallen down.

To be your Comfort,

To be your Guide,

To be your Listener,

Of things you wish to hide.

To be your Friend,

To be your Mentor,

To be your Refuge,

When you want to cry;

So hold His hand,

And trust Him, because He will be there by and by.

By: Christina Carpenter
Written 1/31/00

## PONDER THE WONDERS

Ponder the wonders and beauty of life

How the trees change color,

How the blossoms bloom,

Why wolves howl,

How a tiny cell becomes a human,

How a mother knows to care,

How baby turtles know to go out to sea,

How men come up with life changing discoveries,

How a heart beats,

Why dolphins sing,

How the mind can process information,

How you feel but not see the wind,

How eyes see color, shapes and forms,

How people fall in love,

How land resides on sea,

Why after the rain a rainbow forms,

How the planets revolve around the sun,

How the human body defends itself of sickness,

How people suddenly awake from a comma,

How a star shines so brightly,

Why is it in all these things, we sometimes forget God,

How is it we say we don't see God,

Why is it in all these things we forget to praise God?

By: Christina Carpenter Written 2002

# Day 8

## REMEMBER AND SURRENDER

My every day has become routine

Going about my way

Never stopping to think about God

Just trying to get through the busy day

It's all about what I have to do and the needs I have to meet

Sometimes I give God a little of my time

Only hoping it's enough to please Him.


Yet after a while I'm tired.

Then after a while I'm frustrated.

Then I'm just plain angry.

Why is life such a drag?

Why do I worry and hurt?

Why isn't anything working out right?

Why does God seem so far away?

What am I doing wrong?

Is God even there any more?

In the midst of my despair

I fall to my knees and let go of the reins

—HERE I AM LORD!!

And in this time of humility and jection

God begins to speak,

My child I have told you

"*mit yourself to me. Resist the devil and he will flee.*

"*Seek first the kingdom of God and all these things will be added unto you*"


"*Without faith it is impossible to please me for the one that comes to me must believe that I Am, and that I'm a rewarder of those who diligently seek me*

"*It is not by your might, nor by your power but ONLY by My Spirit*

"*My grace is sufficient for you: for my strength is made perfect in your weakness*

*. . . and last but not least, I have told you . . .*

"*I am with you always, even unto the ends of the earth*"


I wonder in awe at the remembrance of these biblical promises.

They seem so easy to remember and yet I forget.

I hear him speak again, comforting me:

"*Why, my child, have you forgotten the promises I gave you?*

*Have you forgotten that I am here to save you, not condemn you?*

*My child you must remember that I am all you need.*

*You need not go through life alone, because I am the way, the truth and the life; apart from me, you have no life.*

*My child you must remember that no deed you do, will make me love you any more or less, because it is not by your works but by my grace that you are Saved!*

*My child, you must remember, to abide in me and my words abide in you then you can ask what you wish and it will be given to you.*

*I desire for you to grow and learn to be more like me. And most of all remember that I desire a relationship with you,*

*In these things you will find peace for your soul*

*So remember these things and surrender to my will, for it is your heart I seek."*

**By: Christina Carpenter**

## NO BUTS ABOUT IT

Every morning I wake up,

*Thanking God* for another day,

**But** will tomorrow pass my way?

Every morning I look at my family,

And *Thank God* for their safety,

**But** then I think will they really stay ok?

Every afternoon I sit at my work desk,

And *Thank God* for such a good job,

**But** then I think will I get laid off?

Every night I drive in my car,

And *Thank God* for my transportation,

**But** will it be here ten years from now?

Every night I lay in my bed

And *Thank God* to be home,

**But** will I ever loose my house?

Then I look up at the night sky,

And know that there are *no buts about it*,

Because God's in control of all "buts . . ."

Every one I can think of.

By: Christina Carpenter 10/4/98

"For God hath not given us the spirit of fear; but of power, and of love, and of a sound mind." 2 Timothy 1:7 KJV

# PART 2

## WHO GOD IS . . . REFLECTIONS ON THE ETERNAL LOVER

*Reminder: check out the additional reflections at the end of this book in the appendix.*

# $\mathcal{D}ay$ $10$

## ANSWERED PRAYERS

Hands clasped tight, I send a silent prayer

Up into your heavenly realm my voice rings

You hear me, in you majesty, you decide,

Decide whether to respond—"Yes", "No" or "Wait."

Sometimes I receive my request with a yes,

Then I rejoice with gratitude and thankfulness

Songs of praise and dances of joy, God is so good.

Sometimes I receive nothing with a response of no,

My heart sinks all my hope is drowned

I grudge and wonder why not, it doesn't seem right

Complaints, tears, all is lost, God doesn't make sense.

Sometimes I receive nothing yet with a response to wait,

My heart says why, my heart wants it now

My emotions wage within, why is time so long?

Has God forgotten his promises, has he forgotten my needs.

**God in his majesty has the power to choose,**

Has the knowledge to chose, has the wisdom to know what's best,

He said, *My ways are not your ways and my thoughts are not your thoughts.*

Yet I, in my frail, tiny, immortal humanness

Try to understand; try to comprehend, what are his reasons,

Why he chooses to say yes, no or wait.

Sometimes he has to put me in my place,

Reminding me that he is the one who created time, life and space.

By: Christina Carpenter 12/7/02

# *Day 11*

---

## ALL THE REASONS WHY I LOVE THE LORD

You pick me up . . .

You found me . . .

You came to me . . .

You noticed me . . .

And that is why I love you.


No matter how near or far I am

You care enough to be there

You loved me first


When all I knew was lost

In chaos and confusions

In troublesome storms

You and only you calmed them

With Gentle whispers

Your love seemed to take my cares away.

By: Christina Carpenter 2011

---

# *Day 12*

## SPEAK TO ME LORD AGAIN

When am I going to hear you lord?

Speak to me lord I need you.

Tell me what I need to do.

I can't go forward

I can't go another step without you.

Show me your path

Guide me in your truth

Lead me

I'm praying. I'm seeking you.

Please speak

I know you will answer.

By: Christina Carpenter 2011

# *Day 13*

## HIS WONDERFUL PRESENCE

Can it be?

Why is this happening to **me?**

Could he really love me? . . .

—**This much?**

Is it right?

Is it ethical?

The way I just say a prayer

And then wham—

It's T H E R E?

Can it REALLY be?

Be happening to me?

Why—it's amazing.

And—it's so perfect!

I feel I have a secret

That everyone ought to know

But how can I tell it?

Would they be able to believe?

That someone <u>unseen</u>,

Is standing beside me

*Holding* me

*Hiding* me

*Keeping* me

*Loving* me—***unconditionally?!***

Can you fathom?!

Can anyone dare believe?! He's real!!!


No one knows how good this feels!

But me,

I have this infinite powerful God

He's *helping* **me!!!**

Oh my gosh-

—oh my Gosh!!

My mind is blowing at

His awesome love.

Can you imagine it?.


Imagine asking . . . and then

Receiving.

Imagine weeping . . . and then

Smiling.

Imagine sighing and then

Rejoicing.

Imagine fearing . . . and then

Conquering!!!

That's my GOD!!!

He helped me through

What ever I need

He **always** provides

Whenever I'm sinking

He *lifts* me up

All I do is call His name

And he *hears and answers*

Don't be mistaken

By all the things I've achieved,

All the joy and great things that happen,

The peace that dwells inside,

It's not from me

Not from me at all!

I can have none of these things

Without Him.

He's my awesome God

He is a loving God

A merciful GOD

HE IS A WONDERFUL GOD!!!

—And this **I know**.

By: Christina Carpenter

# Day 14

## JESUS, MY ONE TRUE LOVE

I've been looking for my one true love

And realized I forgot about the one above

Been looking for the right one, the special one

Then remembered about God's son

Been looking for the one to put my trust in

And remembered you died because you loved me

Been looking for someone to love me unconditionally

Remembered you were there with me through the thick and thin

Been looking for someone to respect me

And remembered you created me and forgave me

Been looking for someone to share my feelings with

Remembered you were always listening

Counting my tears in a bottle

Been looking for someone to forgive my past

And remembered you forgave it all, as much as seventy times more and more . . .

After thinking this through, time and time again
I realized my one true love
Was always you.

By Christina Carpenter 2001

## LORD, WE LOVE YOUR HOUSE

We love to be in your house!!
How we love your presence.
To tell our hearts
Who is King!

It's not us.
Only you.
Not the people around us.
It's you.

No one else can dictate our rise or fall
But only you.

So our hearts belong to you.
They belong only to you.,
For this is why we love to come into

Your house

To feast at your banqueting table

To sit at your lovely feet

To bask in the radiance of your love

Your Holy unconditional love.

By: Christina Carpenter 2011

# Day 16

## YOU ARE HIGH ABOVE THE MOUNTAINS

You are high above the mountains
Your glory shines above the heavens
Humbled yourself to love and save us
Be praised through endless generations

There is no one like our God
He gave his son for us.
Jesus the lord
Who can love us like he does?
No one at all
And oh how we love you lord

You lift the needy from the ashes
You seat them high up with the princes
You give the barren women healing.
She'll dance with joy.
Like the mother of many children.

By: Christina Carpenter 2011

*Christina Carpenter*

# Day 17

He will never leave you nor forsake you Joshua 1:5

*Fear though not: for I am with thee: be not dismayed; for I am thy God: I will strengthen thee: yea, I will help thee; yeah I will uphold thee with the right hand of my righteousness.* Isaiah 41:10 KJV

## STAND CLOSE (JESUS)

Jesus

Stand close to me

Lead me on my way


Stand close to me

Lead me everyday


Be close

Be close to me!!!


For I . . . I know

I know . . . I know . . . . I know

I can't go on this journey today
Not without you

Be close to me . . . .
Lead me on my way
Be close to me

Each and everyday
Each and every day!!!

Stand close—Stand close

Everyday close
Stand close to me!!!!!

Every day—Day after day! Everyday

Every day.
Because I need you!

By Christina Carpenter

*The lord is my Shepard I shall not want he leadth me beside the still
waters, he restores my soul, Yeah, though I walk through the valley of the
shadow of death, I will fear no evil: for though art with me; thy rod and
thy staff they comfort me. Psalm 23: 1-4 KJV*

# PART 3

## THE QUEST FOR GOD, IN A HARSH REALITY

*Dear friends do not be surprised at the painful trial you are suffering, as though something strange were happening to you. But rejoice that you participate in the sufferings of Christ, so that you may be overjoyed when the glory is revealed. 1 Peter 4:12-13 NIV*

*Seek the Lord while he may be found; call on him while he is near.*

*Isaiah 55:6*

*Reminder: check out the additional reflections at the end of this book in the appendix.*

## HARD TIMES

Though we may go through life's hard times,

God is around He is not blind.

He sees the pain, He sees the struggle,

But there is a purpose behind this big bundle.

Bad things happen and we focus on the pain,

We get so blind we don't see the benefit or the gain,

But then we think how can that be, in something so tragic,

Just a catastrophe?

This is not a game, this is not magic,

The thoughts, feelings and emotions, just keep going at it.

Though you may not see the purpose or the lesson,

God has a plan that will bring you bless'n!!

In the end you will see the benefit and the gain,

That came out of this bitter struggled strain . . .

It may not come now, or straight forward to your face,

But gradually through it you will see God's grace.

By: Christina Carpenter

"Therefore the redeemed of the Lord shall return, and come with singing unto Zion; and everlasting joy shall be upon their head: They shall obtain gladness and joy; sorrow and mourning shall flee away."
Isaiah 51:11 KJV

# Day 19

## FICTIONAL POEM (STORY)
## FREEDOM!!!

Sick!

She was sick of it all!!

Heavy rusted iron chains

Bitter cold and raw

Gripped around her wrists.

Tying and Binding her soul

Making her prisoner

She felt enslaved and her spirit in Hell

Each day, she lived Hell on earth

Living was hopeless torture

Without mercy nor redemption

Freedom!

Freedom was what she wanted

Freedom from the world

From helpless—accusation, jection, mindless squeezing, time pulling
her down
From jackals and lions all roaming and prowling
Waiting to pounce
They leave her frozen and afraid.

She wanted Freedom from this bondage
Freedom from this misery and *this* pain . . .

And That Door, tall and grey-
God sent but
She could not dare reach it
Her arms and legs
Locked and Bolted. Trapped.
The door would stand there for all eternity
It would become her tombstone

And only for her doom,
There written above it,
*"Be Perfect. Be Free."*

But how could she?
How could anybody?
And so—She cried and asked
Who could save her Soul?
For she saw no other way but death.

And at that moment—

In holy chorus rang

A sea of angels in harmony sang

*"Freedom is yours!"*

*There is one, for thee,*

*One who came to set captives free!"*

She sat quietly and listened,

With an open heart she drank in those words

And she believed.

Then in bright light—Appearing and piercing

The darkness fell away

—and a righteous man descended in a cloud of light

Gentle, pure, holy—Oh so Holy

He clutched her hand and instantly her chains fell away

He raised her with Him into glory and splendor.

And she

Looked up to Him

In utter weakness

And she hoped on him—her savoir.

The redeemer of her soul

The giver of life

True life—Without fear and with out demons.

He gave her power, love and a sound mind.

And most of all He gave her freedom;

Freedom to live and smile again,

In hope—in Freedom—her freedom at Last.

By: Christina Carpenter

# *Day 20*

## LAMENTATION FOR A SEASON

Burning fast and shockingly

Through the family portraits clean in frames

All the Crops, Furniture, Money and Home—burned

Fire burned it all.

Now only charred ash blows into an overcast smoke.


A foundation

Formerly laid and planted is now bare

Gone—Up into thin air.


A single farmer,

Standing in despair just watching

He shakes his head in helpless frustration

He drops his hat and kicks it

He can't help but weep and swear.

All his hard work is gone—gone forever.

He shouts to God: "If only He'd had been watching out . . .

If only He'd taken care . . .

If only He'd been there and answered my prayer . . .

This would have never happened!!"


He spits at God now—"Who is God?" This farmer asks.

He vows to disown the God he once knew

The God of love he doesn't understand . . .

Now he asks himself, "Who is the God of love?"

"Life will never be the same," he hollers.

"It is gone. Totally ruined." And The farmer repeats it—over and over.

—Hardening his heart.


But little does the farmer know—God listens

God blows gently in the wind-

Ready to put out the fire

Almost ready to have the seeds once planted grow again

Little does the farmer know—That God is able.


But so little—So very little does the farmer know . . .


If the farmer would only stop and listen

If only he'd hear the comfort

Blowing in the wind

God whispers words of assurance.


IF only the farmer could listen

If only he'd understand and see that
The life—once dead—Will rise again.

If the farmer only would have faith!!
That the dirt and the ash
Will be tossed away; and A rose of Sharon
Will rise and stand in its place

If only he knew
That the God—The God love,
Would show Himself to be faithful and true.

If only the Farmer knew
That God cares about the seeds—
And is ready to make them grow again.

If only the farmer knew
That all would be well
If only-
If only the farmer would trust . . .

And see . . .

That this was only a lamentation—for an appointed season.

By: Christina Carpenter 2004

*Weeping may remain for a night, but rejoicing comes in the morning.*
Psalm 30:5 NIV

# *Day 21*

## I SEE CLEARER NOW

The world's need for God
Is becoming so real and clearer
Everyday the more I see . . .
The more I want to cry and to say . . .
*Jesus, where are you?*
This world scares me, the things I see scare me
I didn't see it much before,
But the world really needs you,
So very, very badly.

In the streets
I see a man and woman fight,
I see the man pull a knife
Why God, why?

At school
Heightened security starts our ways

Yet two kids get slashed in the same day
Why God, why?

On the bus,
A gang fight starts, one boy has a gun
People scream, I'm crying to your son.

I'm so afraid
God where are you?
Come quickly and take me away.
Evil is taking over everyday
I'm tired of sin and corruption
I'm tired of people being ignorant to you.

God I'm so anxious,
Send your son today
Cause the world is dieing
And getting more corrupt by the day,
It scares me, it scares me
Come quickly Lord Jesus . . .
Jesus come quickly.

By: Christina Carpenter 3/2/02

# Day 22

## WHO I REPRESENT

Who do I represent?
Jesus Christ.

In the world of evil, lies, deception
and Gossip . . .
Laughter at evil.
Hate for good and love for unwholesome things

Who do I represent?
My God. The Only God.

I'm an Ambassador.
I can't stay silent
I can't be in the world and of the world
Because **I'm not** of this world . . . I don't want to be.

God said love goodness

and do well

Who do I represent? God.

I am an ambassador

A sweet smelling savor

To his nostrils

I am the head and not the tale.

I don't want to shrink back in fear

I keep my eyes straight and forward to God

No temptation has me yet

It is a serious deal

A life choice

Being the opposite of the majority

Being with God I have authority

To raise the name of my God

In my heart and mouth and mind

All the days of my life . . .

My knee will bow and tongue confesses

Jesus is Lord.

By: Christina Carpenter

# *Day 23*

---

*An allegory poem*

## THERE IS HOPE. JESUS IS LIFE

TAKING HOLD OF HER—The lies of Satan are choking her

Drowning her—Taking away all signs of hope

And cutting off her supply of life.


She gasps for air—She reaches for life, desperately

—But she's not strong enough

THE KING OF ALL EVIL has no mercy

He laughs at her, as she drowns in a sea of despair

Choked on his dangerous poison.


And I watch in horror and I scream-

*Because I too was a **victim**.*


A victim of his hand clutched tight around my neck,

Forcing me lower and lower,

Pushing me deeper and deeper. I gasped for air

---

I struggled for Hope

But—he kept pushing me-

down, deep down into the deep blue of-

Despair.

Loneliness.

Worthlessness.

Meaningless.

Hopelessness.

Anger.

Fear.

Destruction.


I cannot watch him take another victim

Innocent and blind to see the truth

She follows him, and unknowingly believes in him

There is no light to guide her.

Oh, I cannot watch any longer!

Another innocent, victim, blinded to the Truth,

Drowned once again!

I am tired of seeing her drown!!

I am tired of seeing her listen!

Listening to him only to become trapped, even more, into his deadly web

The devil is sly. He's playing the *same* trick every time

And every time another victim is sucked in.


Victims reach out—Grasping for anything—something!

Only to grasp the hand that put them there in the first place.

It happened to me, I too was being swallowed up

I also began to drown,

I reached and grasped,

—But there was a light—*A light from Above*

Because of this light, I was saved

And a hand of might clutched mine

That hand of strength pulled me out

And upwards I flew, free of

Despair.

Loneliness.

Worthlessness.

Meaningless.

Hopelessness.

Anger.

Fear.

Destruction.

I pray SOMEONE would listen, this time.

I Pray SOMEONE will hear the Truth.

Receive the light, the light of all men,

The true Hope, the abundant and

Free giver of Life—**Jesus Christ**.

Satan wants to drown—kill and destroy

*But* Jesus Christ came to help and to save

And He is waiting and is

—Always waiting—HERE—Where you are.

He is waiting to give New Life.

To those who Call on him-

He will save.

By Christina Carpenter 12/28/03

# Day 24

## VICTORY BATTLE AGAINST RULERS OF DARKNESS

In the battle against rulers of darkness,

I fight as a child of God for righteousness

Yet the battle is hard and draining

I feel helpless as the fiery darts, hit me . . . hit me and hit me again.

I fall; but I feel I can't get up . . .

Then I look back up to God,


And I call and call and call

I see no answer, hear no answer, feel no answer.

Where are you? Why am I fighting this alone? I cry . . .


I sit and wait and wait and wait . . .

Then I hear . . . and feel . . . a rumble,

It's calling my name,

Looking around, I see nothing.

I call again, "Here I am!"

Words of life flood my heart, as he replies back with power

*Get up my child, you are mine, I will never leave you*

*Trust me, believe me, I am with you, for you are mine*

I slowly regain my strength inching up to stand tall and fly,

Finally erect with might and power,

I slay the dragon of nefarity,

Satan fades away and leaves behind the tracks of retreating defeat,

As I step forward and claim the already won victory.

I rejoice!


In my savior

It was done through Him.

The Lord Jesus Christ. His death and his resurrection.


By: Christina Carpenter

## THE GOOD SHEEP

Oh, Good Lord, I heard you before, but now silence.

Waiting . . . Waiting . . . Waiting.

How long . . .

For the Good Shepard to lead me on?

I've been in these dark pastures

Just Sitting.

I see green on the other side

But I am waiting . . .


Waiting for the small gentle voice

To show me the way to the other side.


I know the Lord will get me there.

I dare not attempt it alone.

Not till I hear his voice.

By: Christina Carpenter

# Day 26

## NOT MY WILL, BUT GOD'S WILL

You want to
Live in God's will,
His eternal will . . .
Stop being clueless

Stop asking what is God's will
*For me.*
But instead what is God's will
*Period.*
Stop thinking about yourself
It's not all about you.

See God's will through God's perspective
Learn God's story
This is the only way to
Learn God's will.

Learn His will through

His word

What does it say?

Study it

Obey his unequivocal will.

You want to know God's will

Then you will never

know it till your start

Studying it

Thinking about it

Loving it and Living it

Living Gods will in the things you do know

He wants you to

Act with integrity

Make choices prayerfully

When God works in you

It is just as important as

His work through you.

Build integrity by

Practicing it day by day.

By: Christina Carpenter Written 10/28/04

# PART 4

*For you have spent enough time in the past doing what pagans chose to do—living in debauchery, lust, drunkenness, orgies, carousing and detestable idolatry. They think it strange that you do not plunge with them into the same flood of dissipation, and they heap abuse on you.*
1Peter 4:3-4 NIV

*Reminder: check out the additional reflections at the end of this book in the appendix.*

# *Day 27*

## EVIL'S CURRENT

Going up stream against the current

The currents that pull and tug,

The currents of sin and the ways of the world,

Begging you to go with the flow,

Though it would be so easy to blend with the crowd,

But you keep steady and instead cry out "No!"

You must be different from the rest,

To not yield to temptations test,

They beg you to go with the flow,

Still you must keep steady and just say "No!"

You know there is something better,

You know there's a reward to this struggle

So you move on, yes the trail is rough

Though the current seems to sweep you away,

You must keep going, keep pulling, and keep climbing

And You Must!!!

Because the current will tell you to go with the flow,

But you have to keep steady and say just say "No!".

You are not struggling in vain, for Christ said:

Those who are persecuted for righteousness,

Theirs is the kingdom of heaven.

By: Christina Carpenter 4/16/00

# WHERE ARE YOU GOING?

Do you know where you are going?

When life is stolen away,

By that thief who takes the ones who want to stay.

The thief who is coming to your house,

Anticipating to knock on your door,

While you sit and wish time were more.

Do you know where you are going?

Heaven or Hell?

When the door is open and you're in another realm,

Is it regretting or praising that's your song?,

And are you sure that's where you really belong?

BY: Christina Carpenter written 12/25/99

*We are confident, I say, and willing rather to be absent from the body, and to be present with the lord.*

*2 Corinthians 11 5:8*

# Day 29

## THE GREAT RACE

I just learned something . . .

Life is a race

A long traveling journey, across track distance, across deserts

Valleys, Seas, mountains and plains

Filled with highs and lows

All for one purpose

To make you and train you


We all run the race

Yet no race is exactly the same

Each unique to his own runner

Each on a different mission

A different level to prove to our master

That we can do the duty

We can finish our run for the calling on our lives

All at the end we all have it in us

Victory, a winners banner

Yet the glory doesn't come easy

It takes great strength and strides,

A commitment to finish well.

Honestly, all through it you will want to give up

But don't!

That winners circle is waiting for you to jump in feet first!

By Christina Carpenter

## DON'T GIVE UP—RACE ON!

Race on my people, young and old

Don't trip or fall

We have to race on

You can't run someone else's race—just your own

You must see your own journeys end.

And pursue it to the finish line

See the path God has for you

Envision the victory and win

Embrace God who put you there to win it.


Don't throw in the towel

Fight, strive, push and go

Don't stop, till you've made progress.

Keep going

Take a refreshing pit stop if you need to

But don't quit the race

Don't get confused by irrelevancies
These are distractions

Get refreshed in God's word.
God knows what you need
He will give it if you seek him

Remember what you are racing for.
Don't quit.

By: Christina Carpenter

"Wherefore seeing we also are compassed about with so great a cloud of witnesses, let us lay aside every weight, and the sin which doth so easily beset us, let us run with patience the race that is set before us," Hebrew 12:1 KJV

# *Day 31*

## NOTHING RIGHT IN ME

Though I have pushed and struggled to do what is right
I've finally thrown in the towel
Sweat and prayed
Cried and strayed
Lord, nothing ever seems to work
What is wrong with me?
What is not right?
In me . . . ?

Of course only God knows because
You sent your son, Jesus, to give me hope
Sent your son, Jesus to take my burden
I can do nothing without Him
I can be free, but only in Him
I am now free, because of you
I am good in Christ, no matter how wrong I may be.

*Christina Carpenter*

Your son, Jesus Christ came to make me new and true

He came to save me

Now I can rejoice

Because now . . .

There is redemption

There is a Holy Inheritance

There is unconditional love

There is forgiveness

For every wrong in me


There is a father

A friend.

An intercessor.


There is something right.


That right is in your Son, Jesus.

I've finally found that I need you most

Even more than I thought I needed to be right.


By: Christina Carpenter

Written 4/15/06

# *Day 32*

## I QUESTION, THEN GOD ANSWERS

Can someone hear me when I cry out from this open space of loneliness?

This desire that takes no shape or form . . .

I don't know who I am

Or how I will become anything

Or who I am supposed to be . . .

Where does life begin from here?

How do I go on?


I am looking for answers . . .


In this jumble of emotions and confusion in my mind

In this confusion

I confess I feel alone

Who, where, and why am I?

Will I go further?

Why do I hope for something I can't see?

Why do I desire more?

Why am I who I am?

Why am I here?

With all my blessings and gifting

I know I must be blessed

But will God use me

One day

And if so?

When, how, and Why?

The answer is in God's word:

*Do not worry about your life, what you will eat or drink; or about your body, what you will wear . . . Look at the birds of the air; they do not sow or reap or store away in barns, and yet your heavenly father feeds them.* (Matthew 6:25-26 NIV)

*. . . being confident of this, that he who began a good work in you will carry it on to completion until the day of Christ Jesus.* (Philippians1:6 NIV)

*For I know the plans I have for you,' declares the lord, 'plans to prosper you and not to harm you, plans to give you hope and a future.* (Jeremiah 29:11 NIV)

Thank you Lord for your Word!!!

By: Christina Carpenter written 2006

# Day 33

## THE USEFUL, REJECTED SINNER

Why does God pick the most messed up people to be His vessels?

To preach great sermons?

To bring people to a knowledge of Christ?

To write great books and devotionals?


Those who suffer the most pain seem to

To have the most blessing . . .

The most redemption . . .

The most anointed call . . .

The most calm and trust in God.


Can trials make us stronger?

Yes they can

Can they build testimonies?

Yes.

And from the tribulation

Brings forth the diamond in the rough

*Christina Carpenter*

Beautiful men and women of God

Used for His specific purposes

Just the inner core of beauty is all he wants,

While He sloughs away all that is not of Him.

He uses the very one with the problems

To share in the solutions

Just the very lowest in life

To now be the head of the table and at the top of the list

God uses the lowly

For His higher purposes

The chipped and the crippled

The bruised and the broken

He changes them,

The dirty to make them clean

The useless to make them useful.

All for His glory

His majesty and power

To show that He can use anyone

For anything

Whatever the situation Good or bad

He can turn it for His ultimate good

Though observers may not understand it

And even the person being used

May not understand it

But God understands.

He uses the messed up to show His fix up.

Therefore praise him,

God is awesome and is greatly to be praised.

By: Christina Carpenter

Written 5/4/2006

## The Word—What Did It Say To You?

The Word

When you listen to it

When you read it

When you hear it

Seated in the church pew

What did the Word say to you?


Think about it

Ponder the meaning

Don't let it go in one ear and out the other

Don't let it pour in

Then you shake it out—forgotten.

Don't forget it


No!

Let the word melt into you

Like a seasoning

Let it marinate you

Change you.

Condition your mind


Remember what you learned

What did the word say to you?

Remember, what it said . . .


Christina Carpenter

# PART 5

## HOPEFUL DAYS AHEAD

*The one who calls you is faithful and he will do it.*

1 Thessalonians 5:24 NIV

*Reminder: check out the additional reflections at the end of this book in the appendix.*

## YOUR DAY WILL SHINE

Your day will shine
And show it's time,
Just as the Lord has promised.

Don't be discouraged,
The lord sees your pain,
He wants you to be encouraged.

Have hope, and Try to cope,
With the difficulties that life brings,
Because God is in charge and he is your king.

Just think about all those Bible stories and all of what God did!
Hallelujah!
From the Hebrews in Egypt to Elizabeth and Zachariah.
God did miracles in their lives; he can do one in yours!

Just have patience and you will have all the joy.

God has a plan for you.

It just isn't time,

But your day is coming and it's going to Shine!

By: Christina Carpenter

# Day 36

## HOPE FOR TOMORROW

I feel an awakening in my head. I feel a rising.

I feel sudden burst of *Genuine* energy.

Supernatural God given *Joy.*


*Suddenly* . . .

It is coming from *inside* of me

Like well *springs of hope*!

It is springing forth *to life!*

And playing a beat of happiness on the drum of faith!


I feel the beat pulsate through my being

It makes me want to dance

And praise the Lord. Oh for joy

The joy I feel will be here . . .

Soon!

I love my God.

He gives me hope.

Hope for tomorrow.

By: Christina Carpenter

5/31/06

## BE ENCOURAGED—

## THOSE WHO ARE HEAVY LADEN AND SEARCHING

Don't cry another tear

Know that God is your strength,

He is ever near.

He loves you and cares.


Have peace and trust in God to bring you joy.

He up holds you and will guide you daily.

He preserves you.


Sorrow is multiplied

When you run after other gods

But the true God and lord of heaven and earth, He blesses you and keeps you

Look to Him.

He fills your life with Joy, hope, and purpose

In the midst of hardship know that you will see God's glory

In the land of the living.

Live in faith and rejoice in this hope

That hardship brings patience and patience, brings character and hope.


The lord hears your prayers and knows the things you need

The lord God is a comfort and a provider

Wait on the lord He is never to late and never to early.

He knows when to give you the things you need.

Wait.

Hold on to your faith


Bless and praise the lord and be content with what He has given you

Rejoice in His past goodness.

Remember where He has brought you from.

God is faithful and won't let you down.

Walk with him and he will show you the path of life.

And in his presence you will find

Fullness of Joy, forevermore.

Rest your head in his promises,

He will not let you down.

Be encouraged.


By: Christina Carpenter written 11/ 1/02

## STILL LEARNING, STILL GROWING, STILL TRYING TO BELIEVE

I hated life; I had no reason to live,

Then you came and showed me,

You taught me,

That you came to earth to give me a reason,

You told me I was worth dieing for,

You told me I had purpose,

You said that You had plans for me,

That I was unique, with a special gifting,


I once felt I was unimportant and I was worthless,

Then you came and showed me,

You told me that you thought of me often,

You had thoughts for me that out numbered the stars,

You said that I was just as important as anyone else,

You continually reminded me of your truths,

Showing me, who I was, why I am here and where I am going.

And when I doubted, you patiently reminded me again,

That I am loved, I am growing to be more like you,

And that I will one day be all I was meant to be.

By Christina Carpenter

12/7/02

# Day 39

## MY HOPE

My hope is in You!

Though this world is dead
Everything else is meaningless.
God, <u>you and your will and your Word are everything!</u>

You made everything!!

Even,
Who am I, to change that and walk in my own way?
It would be wrong.
I am no body

But I am somebody with you
And all the nothingness in the world
Is something, when you are the center of it all.

I love you Lord!

Having a relationship with you
Is nothing like having an ordinary love relationship

It's even better!
So much better!

I call to you Lord and you love me
In any circumstance I look for your hand and
Always find that your finger print is there.

Thank you.

By: Christina Carpenter
5/16/09

*But in your hearts set apart Christ as Lord., Always be prepared to give
an answer to everyone who asks you to give the reason for the hope that
you have. 1 Peter 3:15 NIV*

# Day 40

## GOD, YOU MAKE IT ALL OK

It's hard to explain, hard to comprehend . . .

How you counsel me in my emotional uprisings.

You send me messages . . . of Your love,
Through family and friends,
You show me how to handle my problems . . .
Through books and tapes,
You give me strength to go on in Your Word
Jesus, who knows where I would be if it wasn't for You,
My very being is still here because of You.

You know what I need exactly when I need it,
Jesus, Your patience and love are so sweet,
They fill me with hope of a new day,
It makes me to stand with my face to the rain,
Nothing is too hard, Jesus, when I trust in you,

You are so loyal, so understanding,

Even when I worry and complain,

Jesus, I love you so much,

Words cannot express the peace you bring,

I know it will be ok, Jesus

One day it will be ok,

You will make everything ok,

I trust you, to make everything ok.


BY: Christina Carpenter 12/7/02

# 40 Days of More, Deep Reflections

Ponderings for every poem, for everyday

## PART 1

Day 1

Reflecting on God's goodness is like a piece of heaven here on earth, what will you do to reflect? What can you do today to slow down and practice worship and praise to God for loving you? Read Psalms 63

Day 2

How do you know God loves you and where do you see his hand of love in your life?

Day 3

What tangible ways today have you seen God's love towards you today? Read Psalms 92

Day 4

Do you feel alone sometimes . . . maybe even this moment . . . take some time to praise God for his presence? Read Matthew 28:20

Day 5

Relish and enjoy God's grace towards you today.


Day 6

What are you feeling today? Tell the Lord and release it into his care. We all go through stuff, no one is exempt. But know that God has it all under his control, he cares about it all. Read 1 Peter 5:7


Day 7

He made it all! What spectacular things leave you in awe?! Write it down so you can always remember how awesome God is.


Day 8

When we (often) forget who God is—this is when we start to worry and fret. So we need to remember and surrender to who he is and things will seem not to bother us.


Day 9

Instead of worrying about something, try to thank God a little bit more.


# PART 2


Day 10

God is sovereign, and whatever he told you. Listen and take it as it is and do what he says to do. Praise God for his answers to your prayer.

Day 11

We love God because he first loved us . . . so why do you love him . . . ?


Day 12

What are you seeking the Lord for? Are your seeking him about anything?


Day 13

There is nothing more exciting than answered prayer. Why not pray today and see God do a miracle in your life!


Day 14

Is Jesus your one true love? How can you make him number one in our life, today?


Day 15

Do you love the Lord's house? Take time to really enjoy God's House. The Church you attend is the lord's house, a place of worship, where believers gather to fellowship. Praise God wholeheartedly with your brothers and sisters in Christ.


Day 16

Sing a song of praise, for how great is our God! His deeds are good and his ways are full of love. Read any chapter in Psalms and testify his love.


Day 17

Remember God is always next to you, as close as your very next breath.

# PART 3

Day 18

Praise God in the solitude of your bedroom or bathroom and trust that God has a plan even in your hard times.

Day 19

What is holding you hostage? What do you need to be free from? Remember Christ came to set us free. No longer slaves to sin.

Day 20

What is God about to do in your life? You may not see it because you're in a season of fire and testing. But what God has could be beyond what you can fathom. Don't give up hope. Your can mourn for a while but remember Joy will come in the morning.

Day 21

What things in the world scare you and how can you show God you trust him to deliver you?

Day 22

Is your life representing Christ or are you representing something else? How are you living for Christ?

Day 23

What has God saved you from? Remember your testimony and tell somebody about it?

Day 24

Do you feel like you are drowning in overwhelming situations today? Then read Isaiah 43:2-3.

Day 25

Are you listening to the Lord? He speaks to those who take the time to listen. Be like a good sheep and settle down to hear him speak to you.

Day 26

Praise God. The Lord works in mysterious ways. Do you know God's will for your life? Pray daily and seek it out so that you can find out. Even though you don't understand what he is doing, God is still working in and through you.

# PART 4

Day 27

Don't give in to the main stream fads, notions and ideas. Be on your guard and walk the straight and narrow with integrity.

Day 28

Which will it be for you, Heaven or Hell? What about your friends? Do they know where they are going?

Day 29

What race are you running? And do you know what your end goal is? Read 2 timothy 4:5-8

Day 30

Don't give up on your gifts, calling, or mission in life. Read God's word and get strength.


Day 31

Ever feel like you can't get anything right? Relax. God has it all under control.


Day 32

What are your dreams and desires in life? Trust God with them. Put hope in his promises.


Day 33

We are all messed up in some ways and have faults that maybe no one knows about but we know and God knows. Thank God he still uses even the least and makes them greater.


Day 34

Glean wisdom, insight and knowledge by reading the word daily. Don't let it fall by the wayside.


# PART 5


Day 35

Shout Hallelujah! Your days of rejoicing are coming soon! Hope is alive in Jesus Christ no matter what circumstances we may face today.

Day 36

What Hope do you look forward to in the days of tomorrow?


Day 37

Sorrow is multiplied when you chase after the things that don't last in the world. Have a relationship with Jesus Christ rooted in Godliness and be encouraged in the fact that it will last.


Day 38

What is your reason for living? Do you know that God loves you?


Day 39

Place your trust and hope in the living Christ with all your heart today and for eternity because he will never change.


Day 40

Remember that He will make it ok. Jesus will make it ok.

# BIBLIOGRAPHY

All scriptures quotations from:

*NIV Study Bible*, Zondervan 2002 edition.

*God's Promises for your every need*, Word Publishing, copyright 1988, 1995 scripture quotations from The Holy Bible, King James Version.